MUSIC DVD CONTENTS

DAY 1 MENU

"Truth Comes from God" Instruction Video

"Truth Comes from God" Instruction Video with Music

"Truth Comes from God" Performance Video

"Truth Comes from God" Lyrics

Scripture Verse (CSB)

Scripture Verse (KJV)

DAY 2 MENU

"Even Better" Instruction Video

"Even Better" Instruction Video with Music

"Even Better" Performance Video

"Even Better" Lyrics

Scripture Verse (CSB)

Scripture Verse (KJV)

DAY 3 MENU

"The Only Way to Heaven" Instruction Video

"The Only Way to Heaven" Instruction Video with Music

"The Only Way to Heaven" Performance Video

"The Only Way to Heaven" Lyrics

Scripture Verse (CSB)

Scripture Verse (KJV)

DAY 4 MENU

"Name Above All Names" Instruction Video

"Name Above All Names" Instruction Video with Music

"Name Above All Names" Performance Video

"Name Above All Names" Lyrics

Scripture Verse (CSB)

Scripture Verse (KJV)

DAY 5 MENU

"God's Love" Instruction Video

"God's Love" Instruction Video with Music

"God's Love" Performance Video

"God's Love" Lyrics

Scripture Verse (CSB)

Scripture Verse (KJV)

THEME SONG

"Breaker Rock Beach" Instruction Video

"Breaker Rock Beach" Instruction Video with Music

"Breaker Rock Beach" Performance Video

"Breaker Rock Beach" Lyrics

TABLE OF CONTENTS

GOD'S ROCK-SOLID TRUTH IN A WORLD OF SHIFTING SANDS
ROMANS 12:2

CHOREOGRAPHY INSTRUCTIONS

These instructions are designed for you, the teacher. If you are mirroring the instruction video, then stand in front of your kids to teach them, they will mirror you and will be doing the motions exactly as we present them.

If you choose to use the performance segments to teach or lead worship, your kids will mirror the performance videos, and that's OK. It doesn't matter if they go to the right or to the left, just so they're together, worshiping God, and having fun.

AUDIO RESOURCES

You can find the songs on the *VBS 2024 Music CD Set* or download them from lifeway.com.

MEDIA RESOURCES

You can find the videos on the DVD in the Leader Guide *or* purchase them for download from lifeway.com.

EDITORIAL TEAM
KIDS MINISTRY PUBLISHING

Chuck Peters
Director, Kids Ministry

Jeremy Carroll
Publishing Manager, VBS & Kids Discipleship

Rhonda VanCleave
Publishing Team Leader

Klista Storts
Content Editor

Sara Lansford
Production Editor

Beth McGill
Graphic Designer

Jennie Ross
Writer
Works with children in Franklin, TN

Send questions/comments to VBS Publishing Team Leader by email to rhonda.vancleave@lifeway.com or by mail to VBS Publishing Team Leader *VBS 2024 Music Rotation Leader Guide* 200 Powell Place, Suite 100 Brentwood, TN 37027-7707 or make comments on the web at www.lifeway.com.

Printed in the United States of America
© Copyright 2023 Lifeway Press®

ISBN: 9781430089872
ITEM: 005846912

We believe that the Bible has God for its author; salvation for its end; and truth, without any mixture of error, for its matter; and that all Scripture is totally true and trustworthy. To review Lifeway's doctrinal guideline, please visit www.lifeway.com/doctrinalguideline.

Unless otherwise indicated, all Scripture quotations are taken from the Christian Standard Bible®, Copyright © 2017 by Holman Bible Publishers. Used by permission. Christian Standard Bible® and CSB® are federally registered trademarks of Holman Bible Publishers.

Every day is an adventure at Breaker Rock Beach, from the morning waves crashing against the shore to evenings filled with bonfires and s'mores! Catch a glimpse of an orca leaping through the surf or watch happy sea lions playing among the rocks beneath magnificent pines. Race along the sand with your brightly colored kite, join friends to make the most amazing sandcastle, or gaze in wonder at the mysteries found in a glimmering tide pool. As the crowds come and go and the tides ebb and flow, Breaker Rock rises majestically as a symbol of strength, standing firm against the force of wind and waves.

The world around us is filled with wonderful, exciting things that are blessings from God. However, the tide of cultural influence often echoes Satan's distorted truth, "Did God really say … ?" The waves of change are small at first and wash over us effortlessly. They beckon us to jump in and swim before we can spot them for what they often are—half-truths or outright lies that can pull us under quickly. But unlike the shifting sands of culture, God's truth never changes. It stands strong like a towering rock—a beacon calling us to hold tight to it so we aren't tossed about by every new crashing wave.

At Breaker Rock Beach, kids will learn to recognize the difference between what the world says is true and what God says is true. They'll encounter five everyday sayings that sound right, but dangerously miss the truth found in God's Word. Each day kids will be challenged to know that God's truth never changes—even when it's radically different from what some people say. They'll discover that God does not want them to be conformed to this age, but to be transformed by the renewing of their minds so that they can discern what is the good, pleasing, and perfect will of God (Romans 12:2).

VBS SCRIPTURE

- Do not be conformed to this age, but be transformed by the renewing of your mind, so that you may discern what is the good, pleasing, and perfect will of God. *Romans 12:2*
- And be not conformed to this world: but be ye transformed by the renewing of your mind, that ye may prove what is that good, and acceptable, and perfect, will of God. *Romans 12:2* (KJV)

Christ Connection:
Jesus is the only way to receive salvation. When we trust Christ as our Savior, He gives us the desire to love God's Word, obey God, and lovingly tell others about Jesus.

Level of Biblical Learning Concept: The truths in the Bible will last forever.

VBS Motto: God's truth never changes!

DAY 1: SATAN TRICKED ADAM AND EVE
(Genesis 2–3)

Adam and Eve listened to Satan's temptation, chose to disobey God, and broke their relationship with God. This disobedience brought sin into the world. God said He would one day send a man to defeat Satan and restore the relationship between God and people. We now know that man is Jesus.

DAY 2: DANIEL CHOSE GOD'S WAY
(Daniel 1)

Daniel and his friends were taken captive by King Nebuchadnezzar of Babylon. They chose to follow God's plan with the foods they ate while being trained in the king's palace. The friends chose to follow God's plan and God gave them knowledge and understanding. The king found the four friends even wiser than the other men who had been working for him.

DAY 3: THE RICH YOUNG RULER
(Mark 10:17-27)

A rich man asked Jesus how to get to heaven. Jesus told the man to go sell everything and then come follow Him. Jesus knew the man cared more for his things than following Jesus. The man went away feeling very sad. Jesus said it is nearly impossible for a rich person to enter God's kingdom, but all things are possible with God. God sent Jesus to make it possible for all people to be saved.

DAY 4: JOHN WROTE ABOUT JESUS
(John 14:1-6; 18–20; Acts 1:9-12)

John was one of Jesus' disciples and closest friends. John wrote an eyewitness account of Jesus' ministry. Jesus taught that He is the only way to have eternal life. Jesus was arrested, tried unfairly, and sentenced to death. He died on a cross and was buried in a tomb. Three days later, He rose from the dead. Witnesses found the stone that sealed the tomb rolled away! Jesus appeared to many people over the next forty days before returning to heaven.

DAY 5: PAUL ENCOURAGED THE EPHESIANS
(Acts 9:1-6; 19:1-10,21-31; 20:1; Ephesians 3:14–4:16)

Paul used to persecute Christians. Then he learned that Jesus is God's Son and began sharing the gospel as he traveled. Paul visited a town named Ephesus, where many people became believers. Later Paul wrote a letter to the church at Ephesus reminding them to show God's love to others whether they agreed with them or not. Paul challenged the people to grow in their relationships with Jesus and to know God's truth.

Day 1   TRUTH COMES FROM GOD

BIBLE STORY

Satan Tricked Adam and Eve *(Genesis 2–3)*

BIBLE VERSE

Do not be conformed to this age, but be transformed by the renewing of your mind, so that you may discern what is the good, pleasing, and perfect will of God. *Romans 12:2*

And be not conformed to this world: but be ye transformed by the renewing of your mind, that ye may prove what is that good, and acceptable, and perfect, will of God. *Romans 12:2 (KJV)*

BONUS VERSE

The entirety of your word is truth, each of your righteous judgments endures forever. *Psalm 119:160*

Thy word is true from the beginning: and every one of thy righteous judgments endureth for ever. *Psalm 119:160 (KJV)*

TODAY'S POINT

Truth comes from God.

BIBLE STORY RECAP

God created Adam and Eve and placed them in the garden of Eden. He told them they could not eat from the tree of the knowledge of good and evil. Satan, disguised as a serpent, came and urged Eve to eat from the tree and become like God, knowing good and evil. Eve wanted the knowledge Satan talked about. So, she took the fruit and ate it. Adam ate it too. When they ate the fruit, they understood the difference between good and evil and immediately felt shame. Disobeying God was a choice to sin. That sin immediately broke their relationship with God. God told them about the bad things that would happen because they sinned. But God also said that one day He would send a man to defeat Satan. We now know that man is Jesus. He would restore the relationship between people and God.

Truth Comes From God

VBS 2024 Day 1
Psalm 119:160

PREP

❏ Watch the Day 1 segments on the Music DVD to learn the music and choreography for "Truth Comes From God."
❏ Study today's Bible story Recap, Bible verse, and Point.
❏ Cue the music to "Breaker Rock Beach."
❏ Cue the Music DVD to the Day 1 menu.
❏ Gather large sheets of gray or black paper and cut them into rock shapes, enough for kids to stand on. On the back side of four rocks, write one of each of the following words: *Truth, Comes, From, God.*
❏ Arrange the rock cut outs on the floor across the front of your teaching area. Be sure the words are facedown.

VIDEO TIP

"Instruction" videos are provided to help *you* learn the songs and prepare to teach. "Performance" and "Lyric" videos are provided for use with your kids if you choose to use them.

WELCOME

- As kids arrive, play "Breaker Rock Beach." Guide kids to stand on a paper rock and dance or do any choreography moves they remember from Worship Rally.

- Show the words to the chorus of "Breaker Rock Beach." Ask the children what breaks against the rocks? *(waves)* Explain to them they are going to do a group "wave." As you point to each child (or group), they will raise their hands in the air and bring them back down. When done quickly across the room, they will form a wave.

- Repeat two to three times, alternating which side of the room starts the wave. Congratulate them on a job well done.

DEEPER DIVE

- Welcome kids to Orca Music at Breaker Rock Beach. Ask how many children have been to a beach or seen a beach in a video? Ask them: Do the waves ever stop? *(no)* What keeps the waves from taking over the land? *(God)*

- Say: In our Bible story today, we learned that God created the world. Because He created it, He is in charge of it. That means He put boundaries in place for the waves. He also gave boundaries for people too. How do we know we can trust what God says? *(Truth comes from God. He does what He says He will do.)*

- Ask kids to turn over their paper rocks and bring any rocks with words on them to the front. Challenge the kids to put the words in order to reveal "Truth Comes From God." Say: Adam and Eve learned the hard way that truth comes from God alone, no one else. When we follow God's truth, we will be standing on the rock of Jesus and we will not be shaken!

READY TO MOVE: "TRUTH COMES FROM GOD"

- Display and read through the lyrics for "Truth Comes From God."

- Walk slowly through the motions for the verses and chorus. Lead the kids to practice the motions a few times.

- Play the performance video for "Truth Comes From God." Encourage kids to follow along the best they can and to have fun while trying.

CHOREOGRAPHY

INTRO

1. While facing forward, raise hands to one side and clap twice. Then clap twice on the other upper side.

2. Lower hands to one side and clap twice. Then clap twice on the other lower side.

3. Repeat steps 1–2.

VERSE

1. ***Everything started:*** Lean to one side with hands up at your shoulders, palms facing out. Bounce hands forward twice, then come to the center and push hands down to your side, palms facing the floor.

2. ***there in the garden:*** Lean to the other side with hands up at your shoulders, palms facing out. Bounce hands forward twice, then come to the center and make a flat circle in front at the waist with palms down.

3. ***with Adam and Eve:*** Lean to the first side with that hand at shoulder height for two bounces, palm out. Then lean to the other side and repeat with the other hand.

4. ***Adam and Eve:*** Repeat Step 3 with both hands on each side, one hand turned 90 degrees in front of the other hand.

5. ***Satan was lying:*** One hand crosses at an angle to opposite side, palm to the back, then comes up to cover your mouth. Repeat with the other hand on the opposite side and cover your mouth.

6. ***tempting and trying:*** Bring one hand to the front in a circular motion back to that shoulder. Repeat motion three times, alternating hands.

7. ***to get them to eat:*** Lean to one side, reach out that hand to pantomime bringing a piece of fruit to your mouth, repeat on the other side.

8. ***get them to eat:*** Repeat step 7 with two hands instead of one, and bounce them twice at the mouth each side.

9. ***The fruit was forbidden:*** Place hands together in front at your waist, then push hands out from your chest, palms crossed facing out.

10. ***the rule had been given:*** Arms come down so elbows touch your waist with palms up at your side, then bring hands together to the front with hands touching, palms up, chest height.

11. ***but they didn't listen:*** Lean to one side, cross hands twice with pointer fingers up, then lean

to other side and put pointer fingers to your ears twice. Then hands come down in front.

CHORUS

1. **You've gotta stand up for truth:** Make a fist with each hand and do a circular motion while taking a small step forward, then clap hands together with flat palms, chest height.
2. **when Satan is lying:** Repeat Step 5 from Verse 1.
3. **STOP STOP STOP:** Push hands out front three times while doing three gallops with your feet
4. **(stop stop stop):** Push hands down three times while doing three gallops with your feet. (Gallops optional.)
5. **'Cause there's no denying:** One pointer finger goes to opposite shoulder then crosses back to the other side, repeat with the other pointer finger.
6. **we all need reminding:** Hands reach out front, palms up, then touch the side of your head.
7. **truth comes from God:** Lean to one side with hands together, flat palms, touching that shoulder twice. Then stand center with arms lifted in a high V, palms facing in.
8. **(truth comes from God):** Repeat Step 7 to the other side.
9. Repeat the intro.

VERSE 2

1. **When you get tempted**: Lean to one side with hands up at your shoulders, palms facing out. Bounce hands forward twice, then push hands out from your chest, palms crossed facing out.
2. **by all those empty:** Lean to the other side with hands up at your shoulders, palms facing out. Bounce hands forward twice, then push hands down.
3. **lies and deceit:** Lean to one side and place the back of that hand to your mouth, bouncing it twice. Repeat on the other side.
4. **(lies and deceit):** Repeat Step 3 with both hands on each side.
5. **God's truth is power:** Drop one hand and raise it to the side as if making a muscle, hold it while repeating this with the other hand.
6. **a mighty tower:** Raise hands over head with fingers touching as if making a shelter. Repeat motion. (Option, kids can do a little jump with each touch above.)
7. **over your enemy:** Push hands down to one side, then center, then the other side.
8. **your enemy:** Repeat Step 7 in the opposite direction.
9. **So in every trial:** Place hands together in front at your waist, then push hands out from your chest, palms crossed facing out.
10. **look to the Bible:** Arms come down so elbows touch your

waist with palms up at your side, then bring hands together to the front with hands touching, palms up, chest height.

11. **'Cause God's word is final:** Keep hands together but raise them to one side twice, then repeat to the other side. Then hands come down in front.

REPEAT CHORUS (2X)

ENDING

Freeze with hands above head in a high V.

FINISH

- Say Today's Point together: "Truth comes from God!"
- Pray, thanking God that we can always trust His Word is truth, and asking Him to help us learn His truth this week at VBS.
- Play "Breaker Rock Beach" as kids line up to leave. Encourage them to do another group wave as they exit the area.

Day 2 GOD'S PLAN IS BEST

BIBLE STORY

Daniel Chose God's Way
(Daniel 1)

BIBLE VERSE

Do not be conformed to this age, but be transformed by the renewing of your mind, so that you may discern what is the good, pleasing, and perfect will of God. *Romans 12:2*

And be not conformed to this world: but be ye transformed by the renewing of your mind, that ye may prove what is that good, and acceptable, and perfect, will of God. *Romans 12:2* KJV

BONUS VERSE

Trust in the LORD with all your heart, and do not rely on your own understanding; in all your ways know him, and he will make your paths straight. *Proverbs 3:5-6*

Trust in the LORD with all thine heart; and lean not unto thine own understanding. In all thy ways acknowledge him, and he shall direct thy paths. *Proverbs 3:5-6 (KJV)*

TODAY'S POINT

God's plan is best.

BIBLE STORY RECAP

Daniel and his friends were taken captive by King Nebuchadnezzar of Babylon. The king ordered that the young men who had been captured should be served the same food and drink as the king and be trained for three years. Then they would attend to the king. Daniel asked if he and his friends could eat only vegetables and water. He wanted to follow God's plan with the foods he ate. Daniel and his friends were healthier and stronger than all the other men who had been eating the king's food! The friends chose to follow God's plan and God gave them knowledge and understanding. The king found the four friends even wiser than the other men who had been working for him.

Even Better

VBS 2024 Day 2

Proverbs 3:5-6

WELCOME

- As kids enter music rotation, play "Truth Comes From God." Lead kids to remember the motions from Day 1 as they review the Day 1 song.
- Welcome them back to Orca Music. Encourage kids to have a seat around the edge of the picnic blanket.
- Explain that the group is going to play a game. Going around the circle, each person will say his name and select an item that begins with the same letter that he would bring with him on a picnic to Breaker Rock Beach.
- Option: If the group is small enough and there is enough time, add in the challenge that each person must remember the names and items mentioned before them.

DEEPER DIVE

- Ask kids to stand. Remove the picnic blanket and form two groups of kids. Lead them to line up behind a "Start" line. Explain that they will run a relay race. The first child in each group will run to his team's filled basket at the opposite end, pick up an item, run back and drop it in his team's empty basket.
- As each child returns an item, he should say the motto, "God's truth never changes!" to the next child in line who will then repeat the process.
- Kids will continue until one team's items have all been moved.
- Lead kids to sit down. Ask the kids to think about the Day 2 Bible story. Ask: "If Daniel and his friends had a day off and went on a picnic, what items would they have packed?"
- Say: "For many of us, this isn't our ideal picnic. We might want additional items, right? But Daniel knew that God's plan is best. He and his friends decided that these foods were even better than what the king would supply because these foods honored God."
- Help kids understand that we can make that same choice in all areas of life, not just what we eat. We should always ask ourselves if our choices are being guided by God's truth.

READY TO MOVE: "EVEN BETTER"

- Read the lyrics of the song. Take a moment to explain that in the first line "This world" means things we may hear from TV, the internet, books, magazines, and more—people who are not following God's way.

- Practice the motions for the first verse and the chorus. After a couple of walk-throughs, play "Even Better" performance video from the Music DVD. Lead the children to practice all the motions with the video.

CHOREOGRAPHY

INTRO

1. Elbows are out to the side, with one hand up and the other hand down, then snap.
2. Switch so the other hand is up and the other hand is down, then snap.
3. Fists to the side making circular motions, like train wheels.
4. Repeat Steps 1–3.
5. Repeat Steps 1–2.
6. Touch your knees, then stand straight.

VERSE

1. ***This world:*** Take both pointer fingers and point to the floor. Then with palms facing forward, make a circle by bringing hands toward each other then up, out and down.
2. ***tells you:*** Fingers from both hands touch your chin, then reach forward, palms up, while step feet apart. Then hands to your sides and bring feet together.
3. ***you can have it all:*** Reach both hands out front and make a fist as you bring them back in, as if grabbing something. Open hands, palms down, and then make a flat circle with both hands at both sides.
4. ***But I can tell you:*** Place one hand on top of the other, flat with palms toward you, bounce hands twice over your heart. Repeat Step 2.
5. ***they are thinkin' small:*** Hands out, slightly spread apart with palms up. Touch fingers to the sides of your head. Then bring hands together in front, palms facing each out, but not quite touching.
6. ***'Cause they don't:*** Lean one side with palms up waist height, then lean other side while turning palms over and cross hands then open.
7. ***know the:*** Bring one hand to the side of your head while leaning to the first side, repeat to the other side.
8. ***life that Jesus gives:*** With palms facing toward you, rotate hands in a circle while moving up above your head. At the top, bring hands down in front with palms up.

PREP

- ❑ Watch the Day 2 segments on the Music DVD to learn the music and choreography for "Even Better."
- ❑ Study today's Bible story Recap, Bible verse, and Point.
- ❑ Cue the music to "Truth Comes From God."
- ❑ Cue the Music DVD to the Day 2 menu.
- ❑ Place a large picnic blanket in the center of the area.
- ❑ Gather 4 picnic baskets. Place examples of different vegetables (real or toy foods) and a bottle of water inside 2 of the baskets. (Put the same number of items in both baskets.)
- ❑ Place the 2 empty baskets at a taped "Start" line on one end of the teaching area. Place the 2 filled baskets at the other end of the room.

9. **But when you have it:** Reach both hands out front and make fists as you bring them back in, as if grabbing something. Open hands, palms up, and make a circle to the side above each shoulder.

10. **it's the only way to live:** Raise hands in a high V, then bring hands down to shoulders. (Optional: feet apart on high V then feet together as hands move down.) Make a big circle with your hands in front, palms forward.

CHORUS

1. **God's plan:** Clasp hands together in front of chest with elbows down.

2. **is even better:** With feet apart, raise one arm straight to the side at shoulder height facing the side with a flat palm, wrists pulled back and fingertips up. The other palm is facing the same direction, touching the first shoulder. Bounce twice then lean forward with hands on knees.

3. **God's plan is even better:** Repeat Step 1, then Step 2 to the other direction.

4. **Even better than whatever:** Repeat Step 2.

5. **you have in mind:** Reach out in front with palms up, then fingers of both hands touch the side of your head.

6. **God's plan is even better:** Repeat Steps 1 and 2 in the opposite direction.

7. **God's plan is even better:** Repeat Steps 1 and 2.

8. **God's plan is even better:** Repeat Step 3.

9. **even better than the best you'll ever find:** Repeat Step 2, then reach both hands above head and bring down to chest with closed fists.

10. **God's plan is even better:** Repeat Step 3.

VERSE 2

1. **So trust the Lord in:** Lean forward with hands together, flat palms, and head looking down. Stand straight with hands to the side and shoulder height with palms up. Repeat.

2. **everything you do:** Hands waist height, palms up, lean to one side, moving hands with you, move hands to the other side and move back again on three beats. Repeat to the other side.

3. **In all your ways:** Bring one arm up over your head in a circle, repeat with the other arm.

4. **let His truth be guiding you:** Bring hands together with flat palms at chest height. Keep hands together and take them straight above your head. Take both pointer fingers straight out in front.

REPEAT CHORUS

ENDING

1. **Even better than whatever you have in mind, God's plan is even better:** Repeat Steps 4–6 in chorus.

2. **Even better than the best you'll ever find:** Repeat Step 9 in chorus.

3. **God's plan is even better:** Clasp hands together in front of chest with elbows down. Reach hands down in front and make a large circle overhead, then pull hands in toward chest, making fists with elbows down and knees bent. Face is looking forward.

FINISH

- Lead the kids in saying the theme Bible verse, as well as Today's Point: God's plan is best! Remind kids that when we follow God's plan, it's better than anything else! Ask for a volunteer to close in prayer, thanking God that His plan is best.

- As kids leave, have them practice Steps 1–3 from the Chorus of today's song.

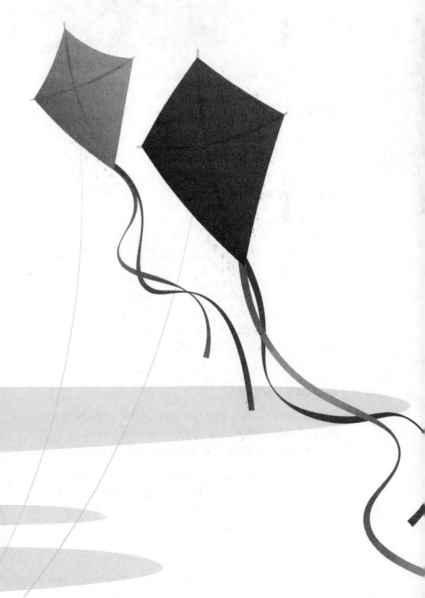

Day 3
EVERYONE NEEDS JESUS

BIBLE STORY

The Rich Young Ruler
(Mark 10:17-27)

BIBLE VERSE

Do not be conformed to this age, but be transformed by the renewing of your mind, so that you may discern what is the good, pleasing, and perfect will of God. *Romans 12:2*

And be not conformed to this world: but be ye transformed by the renewing of your mind, that ye may prove what is that good, and acceptable, and perfect, will of God. *Romans 12:2 KJV*

BONUS VERSE

For all have sinned and fall short of the glory of God; they are justified freely by his grace through the redemption that is in Christ Jesus. *Romans 3:23-24*

For all have sinned, and come short of the glory of God; being justified freely by his grace through the redemption that is in Christ Jesus. *Romans 3:23-24 (KJV)*

TODAY'S POINT

Everyone needs Jesus.

BIBLE STORY RECAP

Jesus is the One that God promised would come to fix the relationship between God and people. One day a rich man asked Jesus how to get to heaven. Jesus reminded the man of God's commandments. The man said he had kept those. Jesus said he needed to sell all his things and follow Jesus. The rich man went away sad. A person does not have to sell everything to get to heaven, but the rich man cared more about his things than following Jesus. Jesus said, "It's easier for a camel to go through the eye of a needle than for a rich person to enter the kingdom of God." The disciples asked, "Then who can be saved?" Jesus said, "It's impossible for human beings, but all things are possible with God." God sent Jesus to make it possible for all people to be saved.

The Only Way to Heaven

VBS 2024 Day 3

Romans 3:23-24

WELCOME

- As kids arrive, play "Breaker Rock Beach." Challenge kids to walk around the room and pick up a shell. Once they have found one, they can come to the center of the room and review the motions while the song finishes.

- When the song is done, welcome kids to Orca Music. Ask kids how many of them have ever collected shells at the beach. One at a time, invite each kid to place his shell in the bucket and share something good he did for someone else that day (or that week). As each child answers, ask him to be seated. Continue until everyone has had a chance.

DEEPER DIVE

- Shake the bucket gently and comment about how many good things are represented by the shells. Say: "These shells represent a lot of good things. What if all these were done by one person? Would that be enough good things for that person to get to heaven?" *(No!)*

- Say: "In today's Bible story, Jesus talked with a young man who followed a lot of God's rules. If he had a bucket of shells for all the good things he had done, I bet it would be a lot like our bucket."

- Distribute the shells back to the kids. Encourage them to work as a group and lay their shells on the ground to form the letters *A*, *B*, and *C*. Explain that the Bible says there is only one way to heaven, and that is through Jesus.

- Display the Day 3 song lyrics and review each letter by looking at the chorus. *(A = Admit to God that you're a sinner and repent. B = Believe that Jesus is the Son of God. C = Confess your faith in Jesus as Savior and Lord.)*

READY TO MOVE: "THE ONLY WAY TO HEAVEN"

- Review the rest of the song lyrics and the motions for each section. Point out that parts of the song stay the same each time, just verse 1 and verse 2 are different.

- Play "The Only Way to Heaven" performance video and encourage kids to join in with you on the motions. If time allows, review the music and motions from Day 1 and Day 2.

CHOREOGRAPHY
INTRO

1. Step to the side while raising one arm up to that side and snap.

2. Repeat to the other direction.

3. Strum an "air guitar" three times, then put hands down to the side.

4. Repeat Steps 1–3.

VERSE

1. *Some people say:* Lift both hands, palms up, to one side. Cup hands around mouth. Repeat both actions.

2. *there's more than one way:* Face the other direction, move hands in a circular motion away from body with palms up for four counts.

3. *to get to heaven:* Push hands palms down to the floor, to the front, and up above. Then repeat Step 3 from opening.

4. *Be kind enough:* Lift both hands, palms up, to one side. Clasp hands in front of chest. Repeat both actions.

5. *show people some love:* Face the other direction, reach out with both hands, palms up. Cross arms across chest. Repeat both actions.

6. *and you'll be OK:* Push hands palms up to the floor, to the front, and up above. Then repeat Step 3 from opening.

PRE CHORUS

1. *But it's not what you do:* Face one direction and make two forward circles with arms, hands in fists.

2. *if it's left up to you:* Repeat that motion in the other direction with palms open.

3. *that only gets you so far:* Drop arms down and lift to other side, with back arm straight and front arm touching far shoulder, both hands with palms facing to the side. Repeat to the other side. Repeat Step 3 from opening.

4. *You know, it's all about grace:* Both hands touch the top of head, then come straight out front, palms up. Keeping straight arms, move hands to one side, then the other.

5. *love, mercy and faith:* Cross arms across chest. Drop hands down and make a large circle above head, and bring palms together at chest.

PREP

- ❑ Watch the Day 3 segments on the Music DVD to learn the music and choreography for "The Only Way to Heaven."
- ❑ Study today's Bible story Recap, Bible verse, and Point.
- ❑ Review the "Sharing the Gospel with Kids" information on the inside cover.
- ❑ Cue the music to "Even Better."
- ❑ Cue the DVD to the Day 3 menu.
- ❑ Gather a sand bucket and enough shells for each child to hold one. (Option: Print shell shapes on cardstock and cut them out.)
- ❑ Hide the shells around the room.

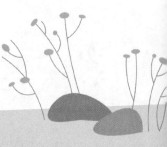

6. **and trusting God with your heart**: Clasp hands, take them down and move out and up in a circular motion. Then lay hands flat on your chest and hold while bouncing to the beat.

7. **to get to heaven:** Push hands palms down to the floor, to the front, and up above.

CHORUS

1. **A – admit to God:** Place both hands by mouth, with flat palms facing out. Push forward twice, then open hands to the side, palms up and head back.

2. **that you're a sinner and repent:** Cross arms in front with each hand grabbing the other elbow, head bent down. Clasp hands together high above head at an angle.

3. **B – believe that Jesus:** Hands together with flat palms by chest, bounce twice. Pointer finger touches palm of opposite hand, then repeat other direction.

4. **is the Son of God:** Cross arms in front with each hand touching the other elbow, as if holding a baby. Raise hands to each side, shoulder height, palms up.

5. **C – confess your faith:** Lean forward bringing both hands to chin, then reaching out front, ending with hands to the side, palms up.

6. **in Jesus as:** Bring one hand over head and straight down with palms back and then up as arms go forward moving slowly all the way down in front. Then other hand repeats so hands face each other at chest.

7. **Savior and Lord:** Both hands go straight up above head and back down. Move hands to shoulder height, palms back, and bring up and forward while bouncing knees.

8. **He's the only way to heaven (Jesus):** Place hands to the side, palms up, and give two pulses upward. One hand goes above head, then the other to form a high V. On "Jesus," bring hands to shoulders, then move hands and arms to a high V. (Optional: jump while hands come to shoulders, then jump again to a high V.)

9. **The only way to heaven (Jesus):** Repeat Step 8.

VERSE 2

1. **Some people say there's more than one way to get to heaven:** Repeat Steps 1–3 from first verse.

2. **Don't lie or steal:** Stack one hand on top of the other, palms down. Push down to one side, bring them up to your face. Repeat both steps.

3. **Make everyone feel good:** Face the other direction, reach out with both hands, palms up. Cross hands across chest. Repeat both actions.

4. **Most every day:** Repeat Step 6 from first verse.

REPEAT PRE CHORUS

REPEAT CHORUS

ENDING

1. **He's the only way to heaven (Jesus):** Repeat Step 8 in chorus.

2. **the Only way to heaven:** Place hands to the side, palms up, and give two pulses upward. Reach hands behind you while leaning forward, continuously shake hands while moving them above head and then back down behind you. (Optional: Continue shaking hands while turning your body in a circle.) End turned to one side with hands reaching up to that side with one arm slightly lower than the other, with flat palms.

FINISH

- Say Today's Point: Everyone needs Jesus. Offer an opportunity for kids to pray and thank God for Jesus.

- Lead kids in a call and response. Say: "A!" Kids respond: "Admit!" Say: "B!" Kids: "Believe!" Say: "C!" Kids: "Confess!"

- Repeat the call and response as kids line up to leave the music rotation.

Day 4 JESUS IS THE ONLY WAY

BIBLE STORY

John Wrote about Jesus *(John 14:1-6; 18–20; Acts 1:9-12)*

BIBLE VERSE

Do not be conformed to this age, but be transformed by the renewing of your mind, so that you may discern what is the good, pleasing, and perfect will of God. *Romans 12:2*

And be not conformed to this world: but be ye transformed by the renewing of your mind, that ye may prove what is that good, and acceptable, and perfect, will of God. *Romans 12:2 KJV*

BONUS VERSE

There is salvation in no one else, for there is no other name under heaven given to people by which we must be saved. *Acts 4:12*

Neither is there salvation in any other: for there is none other name under heaven given among men, whereby we must be saved. *Acts 4:12 (KJV)*

TODAY'S POINT

Jesus is the only way.

BIBLE STORY RECAP

John was one of Jesus' disciples and closest friends. John wrote a book about what he had seen and heard. Jesus often told the disciples that He would be killed, but after three days He would be alive again. Jesus explained that He is the only way to have eternal life. Jesus was arrested and put on trial, then sentenced to death. Jesus was taken to a nearby hillside and nailed to a cross. After Jesus died, He was buried and a large stone was rolled across the opening of the tomb. Three days later, some women walked to the tomb. The stone was rolled away and the tomb was empty! Jesus is alive! Over the next forty days, many people saw the risen Jesus, talked with Him, and even ate with Him. Finally, Jesus returned to heaven.

Name Above All Names

VBS 2024 Day 4

Acts 4:12

♩=94 **Acoustic Ballad**

Words and music by Jeremy Johnson and Paul Marino.

WELCOME

- Greet the kids as they arrive. Show them how to gently blow under their silk scarf (or tissue) to make it float in the air. Give each kid a scarf (or tissue). Play "The Only Way to Heaven" while they walk around the room blowing under their scarves/tissues so they float in the air.

- Welcome kids back to Orca Music. Ask if they have ever seen someone fly a kite at the beach (or seen puffy white clouds at the beach). Comment that the floating scarves can remind us of a sky full of colorful kites (or floating tissues look like puffy clouds).

- Stand in front of the kids and have them mirror your actions while holding their scarves or tissues in one hand. Example: wave it high in the air, move it in a large circle, zigzag it up and down. Lastly, sit down and place the scarf or tissue in your lap.

DEEPER DIVE

- Say: "John wrote about Jesus and his words are in the Bible for us to read. I wonder if John ever looked up into the sky while he wrote those words. John saw Jesus go up into the sky, even higher than a kite (or cloud) at the beach. I imagine that was something John never forgot!"

- Lead kids to pair up and write letters in the air with the scarves. They can challenge each other to guess the letters written.

- Remind kids of Today's Point: Jesus is the only way. Encourage kids to use their scarves or tissues and write the letters of J-E-S-U-S in the air with them.

READY TO MOVE: "NAME ABOVE ALL NAMES"

- Display the lyrics to "Name Above All Names." Draw attention to the first and last lines of verse 2: When all other ground is shifting sand. Request a volunteer to slowly turn the water bottle of sand up and down. Ask the kids to describe what is happening to the sand.

- Ask: "Does this sand look solid?" *(No!)* "According to the Bible, what's a better thing to stand on?" *(solid rock of Jesus)*

- Show the motions for both verses and the chorus. Play the performance video for "Name Above All Names." If time allows, play the performance video of one or two of the previous songs.

CHOREOGRAPHY
INTRO

1. With one hand, palm down, go across the body at waist height while stepping to the side. Then turn the hand up, taking it back across the body with the palm up and hold it at shoulder height, palm up while stepping back together. Continue to hold that hand while repeating the motion with the other hand.

2. Repeat the hand motions above at the same time, taking hands into a large circle above your head and ending with arms down to the sides.

VERSE

1. *There's a name:* Cross the pointer and middle finger of one hand with the pointer and middle finger of the other hand, touching at the middle knuckles (ASL for name). Hold this sign while moving hands down, then out in front.

2. *above all other names:* Hold flat hands, palms down, fingers toward each other at chest height. Then move hands up to forehead height. Hands straight above head with palms forward, moving slowly all the way down in front.

3. *There's a King above all other kings:* Move one hand to the side of the top of head to form half a "crown." Hold it while moving the other hand up to complete the "crown." Take hands into a high V, then hands straight above head with palms forward, moving slowly all the way down in front.

4. *Who is seated:* Push both hands with palms down to one side, with a bend in the knees. Repeat to the other side.

5. *in the highest place:* Reach out with one hand, palm out, across and over in a circle back to your side. Repeat to the other side.

6. *There's a name above all other names:* Repeat Steps 1 and 2.

CHORUS

1. *Jesus:* Pointer finger touches palm of opposite hand, then repeat other direction. (ASL for Jesus). Step to the side and circle hands palms out above head then down to your sides.

2. *His name is Jesus:* Cross the pointer and middle finger of one hand with the pointer and middle finger of the other hand, touching at the

middle knuckles (ASL for name). Repeat ASL sign for Jesus to the other side.

3. *Glorious Jesus:* Hands go to a high V while feet step out, then bring feet and hands back in. Do the ASL sign for Jesus above head, then bring hands down in front, palms up.

4. *Name above all names:* Repeat Step 1 from verse (ASL for name). Repeat the first half of Step 2 in verse, then push hands out in front, palms facing forward, then out to side, ending with hands down.

VERSE 2

1. *When all other ground is shifting sand:* With hands at waist height, palms down, circle them out in front to the other side, then circle back. (Optional: feet can move like on shifting sand. On "sand," one foot steps back while hands move forward together, palms down.)

2. *There's no other place where we can stand:* Push one hand, palm down to the side twice. Repeat on other side. Then, push both hands down together in front. (Optional: Step to one side while pushing one hand down, palm down, to that side twice. Repeat to the other side. Feet jump together while both hands push down together in front.)

3. *He's the solid rock:* Hit one fist into the palm of the other hand. Repeat, switching hands.

4. *the "Great I Am":* Bring both hands to one shoulder, palms out. Push hands up toward the opposite side at an angle. Repeat motion to the other side.

5. *When all other ground is shifting sand:* Repeat Step 1 of Verse 2.

REPEAT CHORUS (2X)

ENDING

Name above all names: Repeat Step 4 in the chorus. Drop head down, then slowly raise head to look up.

FINISH

Pray and ask God to help us remember that He is our solid rock when all other ground is shifting sand. Have kids wave their scarves or tissues in the air as they repeat Today's Point back to you while they line up to leave. Collect the scarves/tissues as they walk out.

Day 5

SPEAK THE TRUTH IN LOVE

BIBLE STORY

Peter Encouraged the Ephesians *(Acts 9:1-6; 19:1-10,21-31; 20:1; Ephesians 3:14–4:16)*

BIBLE VERSE

Do not be conformed to this age, but be transformed by the renewing of your mind, so that you may discern what is the good, pleasing, and perfect will of God. *Romans 12:2*

And be not conformed to this world: but be ye transformed by the renewing of your mind, that ye may prove what is that good, and acceptable, and perfect, will of God. *Romans 12:2* (KJV)

BONUS VERSE

But speaking the truth in love, let us grow in every way into him who is the head—Christ. *Ephesians 4:15*

But speaking the truth in love, may grow up into him in all things, which is the head, even Christ. *Ephesians 4:15* (KJV)

TODAY'S POINT

Speak the truth in love.

BIBLE STORY RECAP

Paul persecuted Christians before he learned that Jesus is God's Son. After that, Paul worked to tell people about Jesus. Paul visited a town named Ephesus. God did amazing things there. Many people became believers and stopped worshiping idols. Those who still worshiped idols became upset, and there was an angry fight in the city. Later Paul wrote a letter to the church at Ephesus. Paul knew what life was like there. Believers in Jesus were persecuted, and people taught wrong things about Jesus. Paul reminded the believers that God loved them. He said believers should show God's love to others whether they agreed with them or not. Paul challenged the people to grow in their relationships with Jesus so that they would know God's truth and not be easily fooled.

God's Love
VBS 2024 Day 5
Ephesians 4:15

- ❏ Watch the Day 5 segments on the Music DVD to learn the music and choreography for "God's Love."
- ❏ Study today's Bible story Recap, Bible verse, and Point.
- ❏ Cue the CD to "Truth Comes From God."
- ❏ Cue the Music DVD to the Day 5 menu.
- ❏ Gather a Bible, a strong flashlight, and enough kazoos to have one per kid.

KAZOO NOTE

Do not reuse kazoos between groups. Provide a new kazoo for each child.

WELCOME

- As kids arrive, distribute a kazoo to each kid. Play the song "Truth Comes From God," and instruct kids to move around the area and play their kazoos along with the music. When the song is over, congratulate the kids on a job well done.

- Gather the kids into a circle and tell them their next task is to make the sound of a foghorn on their kazoos. Have them practice this several times. Ask them where a person might hear a foghorn and why. *(from a lighthouse, to protect ships from hitting the rocks or the shore)*

- Ask: Do you think a ship wants to hear a foghorn? *(No, it means it's in danger.)* Is the foghorn being mean or rude to the ships when it warns them? *(No!)* Should the ship be thankful to the foghorn? *(Yes, it helped the ship.)*

- Have the kids make their foghorn sounds one more time. Then collect the kazoos.

DEEPER DIVE

- Pull out the flashlight and ask the kids where a foghorn is most often found. *(at a lighthouse)* Say: Just like the foghorn, the light from a lighthouse is used to warn the ships of the approaching shoreline. It's there to protect them and help point them in the right direction. It's a light in the darkness for them.

- Pick up the Bible and explain that God's Word is like the foghorn and lighthouse. It is a light in the darkness for us, warning us of approaching dangers and pointing us in the right direction. Help kids see that when we share God's Word with others in a loving way, we are giving them light in their darkness.

READY TO MOVE: "GOD'S LOVE"

- Display the lyrics. Point out the line "It's our only rescue where we can find our refuge." Remind the kids that we find our refuge in God.

- Demonstrate the motions for the song. Lead the kids to practice the motions with you. Play the "God's Love" performance video from the Music DVD. Lead the children to practice all the motions with the video. Repeat the video. As time allows, play the performance video for another song to review it.

CHOREOGRAPHY
INTRO

1. Turn head to face one side, raising that arm straight at an upward angle. Other hand is pointed to the back of your head. Pulse up two times in that position.

2. Clap hands behind back, then in front.

3. Repeat Step 1 to the other direction, then repeat Step 2.

4. Repeat Steps 1–3.

VERSE

1. ***God's love is like a rock:*** With elbows at waist, place palms up in front, then cross arms on chest with hands in fists (ASL for love). Then hit one fist into the other palm.

2. ***that stands above the waves:*** Place one hand, palm down at waist level. Other hand goes above at chest level, palm down. First hand goes above at head level, palm down. Both hands move to the side in a wave like motion.

3. ***His love, it never moves:*** Repeat the sign for love, one arm at a time. Arms shoot down to a low V while feet jump apart, then feet jump back together and arms go down at sides.

4. ***it never:*** One hand comes to waist level in front, palm down elbow out, then reverses direction. Repeat with the other hand.

5. ***bends or breaks:*** With hands remaining at your sides, bend at the waist to one side. Then bring hands together to bend an imaginary stick in front over a bent knee.

6. ***What a truth we can cling to:*** Hands go straight up to one side, then bring them down to chest level, elbows down with hands in fists under chin. Repeat to the other side. Hands come straight down.

7. ***It's our only rescue:*** Hands reach out front and pull in as if pulling a rope, one hand at a time. Alternate hands in this motion three times. Arms come straight down to sides.

8. *where we can find our refuge:* Arms reach behind and come up straight over head, ending with arms crossed in front, elbows out and hands holding opposite elbow. Head looks down.

9. *every day:* Hands open up at waist level, palms up. Close back and then open again at chest level, palms up. Close back and open again at above head in a high V, bringing arms slowly down to sides.

CHORUS

1. *It's not the kind of love:* Push one hand down to the side palm down, twice.

2. *the world talks about:* Raise both hands to that side, chin level, then open and close hands. Repeat straight to the front, then repeat to the other side.

3. *It's not the kind that:* Repeat Step 1 to the other side.

4. *we can do without:* Put hands straight down on the side of your legs. Draw them up to your shoulders, and place hands to the side with palms up and shrug shoulders.

5. *God's love:* Push one hand up to the side at an angle. The other elbow goes up to the side at shoulder height. The first elbow repeats that motion. Both arms cross in front (ASL for love).

6. *God's love:* Repeat Step 5 starting in the opposite direction.

7. *It's the kind of love:* Push one hand up to the side at an angle, twice.

8. *that never lets you go:* Cross arms with each hand holding the other elbow, raise it to one side. Then raise to the front and raise to the other side.

9. *It's the kind of love:* Repeat Step 7 to the other direction.

10. *we need to show:* Hands start low and cross in front as they raise above head in a large circular motion.

11. *God's love:* Repeat Step 5.

12. *God's love:* Repeat Step 6.

REPEAT VERSE

REPEAT CHORUS

ENDING

God's love
God's love

Jump feet apart and arms cross over chest for love with head looking up.

EVERYDAY SUPPLIES

❏ Bible

❏ Markers

❏ *VBS 2024 Media Set* (9781430096665)

❏ Music source

❏ Choreography DVD (included in this leader guide)

❏ TV and DVD player

❏ Lyrics poster—Create a poster for each day with the lyrics to each song.

DAY 1

❏ Gray or black paper

❏ Scissors

DAY 2

❏ Picnic blanket

❏ 4 picnic baskets

❏ Examples of different vegetables (real or toy foods)

❏ 2 bottles of water

DAY 3

❏ Sand bucket

❏ Shells (1 per child)

❏ Option: Print shell shapes on cardstock

DAY 4

❏ Small silk scarves (1 per child)

❏ Option: Tissue paper instead of scarves

❏ Empty water bottle

❏ Sand

DAY 5

❏ Bible

❏ Strong flashlight

❏ Kazoos (1 per child)

DECORATING ORCA MUSIC

• Attach the appropriate *VBS 2024 Rotation Sign* (9781430089957) to the door.

• Position a *VBS 2024 Theme Flying Banner with Stand* (9781430089063) on either side of the door.

• Hang *VBS 2024 String Flags* (9781430089049) from the ceiling.

• Position *VBS 2024 Floor Prints* (9781430089056) on the floor to mark a place on the floor for each child to stand.

• See *VBS 2024 Decorating Made Easy* (9781430090120) for more ideas.

LYRIC DISPLAY

Incorporate the display of lyrics into the decorations for Orca Music. Choose a method from the list below.

• Display the song lyrics from the Music DVD included with this guide. All you need is a TV and a DVD player. Each daily song is synced to music on the DVD, meaning all you have to do is simply select the song, sing, and move along!

• Use a computer attached to large monitors, a television, or data projector to display the lyrics from the presentations available on the *VBS 2024 Media Set* (ROM content is accessible only via a computer with a DVD drive).

• Write the lyrics on sheets of poster board or on large sheets of paper. Display the posters on the focal wall during each session.

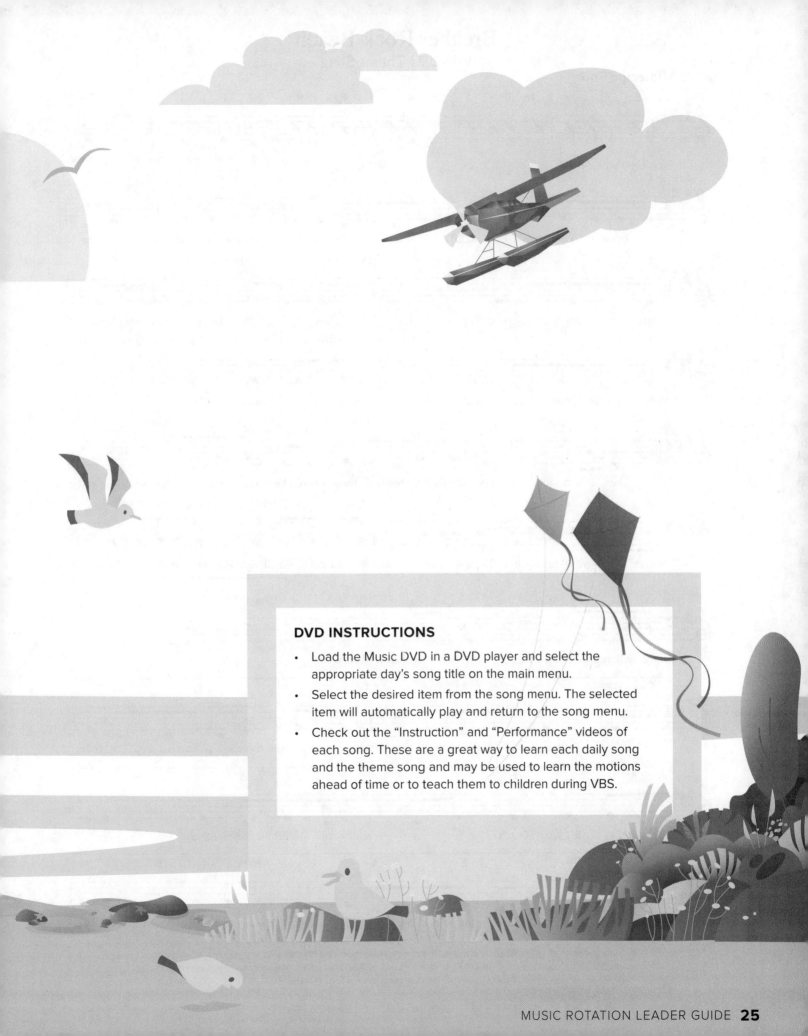

DVD INSTRUCTIONS

- Load the Music DVD in a DVD player and select the appropriate day's song title on the main menu.
- Select the desired item from the song menu. The selected item will automatically play and return to the song menu.
- Check out the "Instruction" and "Performance" videos of each song. These are a great way to learn each daily song and the theme song and may be used to learn the motions ahead of time or to teach them to children during VBS.

Breaker Rock Beach
VBS 2024 Theme Song
Romans 12:2

Words and music by Jeremy Johnson and Paul Marino.
© Copyright 2023 Van Ness Press, Inc. (ASCAP) (admin. by Lifeway Worship c/o Music Services, www.musicservices.org).

Do not be con - formed - to this age,___ but be trans - formed___ by the re-

new - ing of your mind so that you___ may dis - cern___ what is the

good,   pleas - ing,   and per - fect will___ of God.___

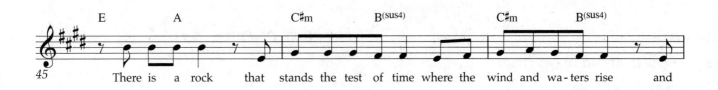

There is a rock   that stands the test of time where the wind and wa - ters rise   and

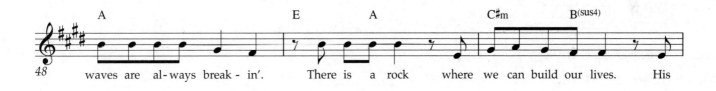

waves are al - ways break - in'.   There is a rock   where we can build our lives.   His

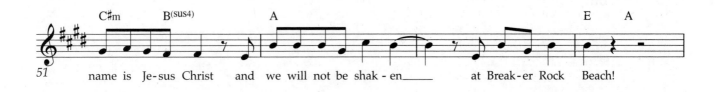

name is Je - sus Christ   and we will not be shak - en___ at Break - er Rock   Beach!

Break - er Rock   Beach!   Break - er Rock   Beach!

TRUTH COMES FROM GOD

(Psalm 119:160)

VERSE 1
Everything started
There in the garden
With Adam and Eve ...
Adam and Eve

Satan was lying,
Tempting and trying
To get them to eat ...
Get them to eat

The fruit was forbidden
The rule had been given
But they didn't listen

CHORUS
You've gotta stand up for truth
When Satan is lying
STOP STOP STOP
(Stop stop stop)

Cause there's no denying
We all need reminding ...
TRUTH COMES FROM GOD
(Truth comes from God)

VERSE 2
When you get tempted
By all those empty
Lies and deceit ...
Lies and deceit

God's truth is power,
A mighty tower
Over your enemy ...
Your enemy

So in every trial
Look to the Bible
'Cause God's Word is final

REPEAT CHORUS (2x)

EVEN BETTER

(Proverbs 3:5-6)

VERSE 1

This world tells you
You can have it all
But I can tell you
They are thinkin' small
'Cause they don't know the
Life that Jesus gives
But when you have it
It's the only way to live

CHORUS

God's plan is even better
God's plan is even better
Even better than whatever you have in mind
God's plan is even better

God's plan is even better
God's plan is even better
Even better than the best you'll ever find
God's plan is even better

VERSE 2

So trust the Lord in
Everything you do
In all your ways
Let His truth be guiding you

REPEAT CHORUS

ENDING

Even better than whatever you have in mind
God's plan is even better
Even better than the best you'll ever find
God's plan is even better

THE ONLY WAY TO HEAVEN

(Romans 3:23-24)

VERSE 1

Some people say

There's more than one way

To get to heaven

Be kind enough

Show people some love

And you'll be OK

But it's not what you do

If it's left up to you

That only gets you so far

You know, it's all about grace

Love, mercy, and faith

And trusting God with
your heart

To get to heaven ...

CHORUS

A – admit to God that you're a sinner and repent

B – believe that Jesus is the Son of God

C – confess your faith in Jesus as Savior and Lord

He's the only way to heaven (Jesus)

The only way to heaven (Jesus)

VERSE 2

Some people say

There's more than one way

To get to heaven

Don't lie or steal

Make everyone feel good

Most every day

But it's not what you do

If it's left up to you

That only gets you so far

You know, it's all about grace

Love, mercy, and faith

And trusting God with
your heart

To get to heaven ...

REPEAT CHORUS

ENDING

He's the only way to heaven (Jesus)

The only way to heaven

NAME ABOVE ALL NAMES

(Acts 4:12)

VERSE 1

There's a name above all other names

There's a King above all other kings

Who is seated in the highest place

There's a name above all other names

CHORUS

Jesus

His name is Jesus

Glorious Jesus

Name above all names

VERSE 2

When all other ground is shifting sand

There's no other place where we can stand

He's the solid rock, the "Great I Am"

When all other ground is shifting sand

REPEAT CHORUS (2x)

ENDING

Name above all names

GOD'S LOVE

(Ephesians 4:15)

VERSE 1

God's love is like a rock
That stands above the waves
His love, it never moves
It never bends or breaks

What a truth we can cling to
It's our only rescue
Where we can find our refuge
Every day

CHORUS

It's not the kind of love the world talks about
It's not the kind that we can do without
God's love
God's love

It's the kind of love that never lets you go
It's the kind of love we need to show
God's love
God's love

VERSE 2

God's love is like a rock
That stands above the waves
His love, it never moves
It never bends or breaks

What a truth we can cling to
It's our only rescue
Where we can find our refuge
Every day

REPEAT CHORUS

ENDING

God's love
God's love

BREAKER ROCK BEACH

(Romans 12:2)

VERSE 1

Take a walk along the coast
Sand beneath your toes
Take it all in, come on let's go
Breaker Rock Beach

See the tall majestic pines
Endless shorelines
Never know what you're gonna find
Breaker Rock Beach

CHORUS

There is a rock
That stands the test of time
Where the wind and waters rise
And waves are always breakin'

There is a rock
Where we can build our lives
His name is Jesus Christ
And we will not be shaken …
At Breaker Rock Beach!

VERSE 2

When you're tempted and you're tried
By the storms of life
There's a place that you can hide
Breaker Rock Beach

In a world of shifting sand
On Christ we stand!
He's the only perfect plan
Breaker Rock Beach

REPEAT CHORUS

BRIDGE

Do not be conformed to this age
But be transformed by the renewing of your mind
So that you may discern
What is the good, pleasing, and perfect will
of God

REPEAT CHORUS

ENDING

Breaker Rock Beach!
Breaker Rock Beach!

NOTES

NOTES

NOTES